God's Open Arms

Studies on Grace

Max Lucado

General Editor

Cover Art by Koechel Peterson and Associates, Inc., Minneapolis, Minnesota. Interior design and composition by Design Corps, Batavia, IL.

Produced with the assistance of the Livingstone Corporation. Study questions written by Christopher Hudson, Carol Smith, and Valerie Weidemann.

ISBN 0-8499-5425-8

99 00 01 02 03 QPV 5 4 3 2 1

Contents

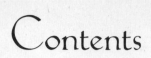

Introduction:

I have good news and bad news.

Let's get the bad news out of the way: We are separated from God by sin. We aren't strong enough to remove it. We aren't good enough to erase it. We can't do enough good deeds to cover it up.

Now here's the good news: God has done what we can't. Before we even recognized our sinful state, he paid the price for what we've done and what we'll do. Jesus was "not guilty, but he suffered for those who are guilty to bring you to God" (1 Peter 3:18).

Ponder the achievement of God. He doesn't condone our sin; nor does he compromise his standard. Rather than dismiss our sin, he assumes our sin and, incredibly, sentences himself. God's holiness is honored. Our sin is punished. And we are redeemed. God is still God. The wages of sin is still death. And we are made perfect.

That's his grace. And that is the best news of all.

—*Max Lucado*

Tough Love, Tough Grace

"We have to see the mess we are in before we can appreciate the God we have. Before presenting the grace of God, we must understand the wrath of God."—Max Lucado

1. How would you describe God's grace to a child?

_____

_____

_____

_____

_____

_____

_____

_____

A Moment with Max

Max shares these insights with us in his book *In the Grip of Grace*.

Many don't understand God's anger because they confuse the wrath of God with the wrath of man. The two have little in common. Human anger is typically self-driven and prone to explosions of temper and violent deeds. We get ticked off because we've been overlooked, neglected, or cheated. This is the anger of man. It is not, however, the anger of God.

God doesn't get angry because he doesn't get his way. He gets angry because disobedience always results in self-destruction. What kind of father sits by and watches his child hurt himself?

What kind of God would do the same? Do we think he giggles at adultery or snickers at murder? Do you think he looks the other way when we produce television talk shows based on perverse pleasures? Does he shake his head and say, "Humans will be humans"?

I don't think so. Mark it down and underline it in red. God is rightfully angry. God is a holy God. Our sins are an affront to his holiness. His eyes "are too good to look at evil; [he] cannot stand to see those who do wrong" (Habakkuk 1:13).

God is angry at the evil that ruins his children.

2

2. Describe in your own words the difference between God's anger and human anger.

_____

_____

_____

_____

3. When have you seen righteous anger?

_____

_____

_____

_____

A Message from the Word

[18] God's anger is shown from heaven against all the evil and wrong things people do. By their own evil lives they hide the truth. [19] God shows his anger because some knowledge of him has been made clear to them. Yes, God has shown himself to them. [20] There are things about him that people cannot see—his eternal power and all the things that make him God. But since the beginning of the world those things have been easy to understand by what God has made. So people have no excuse for the bad things they do.

Romans 1:18–20

4. What does the world around us teach us about God's character?

_____

_____

_____

_____

_____

5. What does it mean that a God powerful enough to destroy us, loves us enough to discipline us?

_____

_____

_____

_____

_____

_____

6. Compare God's discipline to the way a parent disciplines a child.

_____

_____

_____

_____

_____

More from the Word

[1] "Come, let's go back to the Lord.
   He has hurt us, but he will heal us.
   He has wounded us, but he will bandage our wounds.
[2] In two days he will put new life in us;
   on the third day he will raise us up
   so that we may live in his presence [3] and know him.
Let's try to learn about the Lord;
   He will come to us as surely as the dawn comes.
He will come to us like rain,
   like the spring rain that waters the ground."

Hosea 6:1–3

7. What feelings or attitudes keep us from returning to God after we have suffered the consequences of our own sin?

_____

_____

_____

_____

_____

8. If we know that sin destroys us, why do we keep on sinning?

_____

_____

_____

_____

_____

_____

9. In what ways does God's anger lead us to his grace?

_____

_____

_____

_____

_____

_____

My Reflections

"The question is not, 'How dare a loving God be angry?' but rather, 'How could a loving God feel anything less?'"—Max

Journal

In what area of my life have I experienced God's righteous anger as well as his grace?

_____

_____

_____

_____

_____

_____

_____

_____

_____

_____

_____

_____

_____

_____

_____

_____

For Further Study

To learn more about God's attitude toward sin in our lives, read Exodus 20:4–6; Nehemiah 9:16–27; Psalm 66:16–20; Mark 9:45–48.

Additional Questions

10. List some ways that God disciplines us to keep us from sin.

_____

_____

_____

_____

_____

_____

11. In the last few weeks, how has God helped you resist temptation?

_____

_____

_____

_____

_____

_____

12. In what practical ways can we help others understand God's grace?

_____

_____

_____

_____

_____

Additional Thoughts

_____

9

_____

_____

_____

_____

_____

_____

_____

_____

The Manufacturer's Guarantee

"*If we don't acknowledge God, we are flotsam in the universe. At best we are developed animals. At worst we are rearranged space dust.*"

—*Max Lucado*

11

1. If someone told you that humanity is not worth any more than the sum total of the chemicals required to form our bodies, how would you respond?

_____

_____

_____

_____

_____

_____

A Moment with Max

Max shares these insights with us in his book *In the Grip of Grace.*

With God in your world, you aren't an accident or an incident; you are a gift to the world, a divine work of art, signed by God.

One of the finest gifts I ever received is a football signed by thirty former professional quarterbacks. There is nothing unique about this ball. For all I know it was bought at a discount sports store. What makes it unique is the signatures.

The same is true with us. In the scheme of nature Homo sapiens are not unique. We aren't the only creatures with flesh and hair and blood and hearts. What makes us special is not our bodies but the signature of God on our lives. We are his works of art. We are created in his image to do good deeds. We are significant, not because of what we do, but because of whose we are.

2. Why do people tend to define themselves by what they do?

_____

_____

_____

_____

_____

3. What evidence of God's signature do you see on your life?

_____

_____

_____

_____

_____

A Message from the Word

¹³ You made my whole being;
    you formed me in my mother's body.
¹⁴ I praise you because you made me in an amazing and
      wonderful way.
    What you have done is wonderful.
    I know this very well.
¹⁵ You saw my bones being formed
    as I took shape in my mother's body.
When I was put together there,
    ¹⁶ you saw my body as it was formed.
All the days planned for me
    were written in your book
    before I was one day old.

Psalm 139:13–16

13

¹⁰ God has made us what we are. In Christ Jesus, God made us to do good works, which God planned in advance for us to live our lives doing.

Ephesians 2:10

4. What parts of creation most convince you that there is a Creator?

_____

_____

_____

_____

_____

_____

5. Why is it sometimes difficult to value ourselves as God's creation?

_____

_____

_____

_____

_____

_____

6. What difference does it make in your everyday life to know that God has ordained all of your days?

_____

_____

_____

_____

_____

_____

_____

More from the Word

[21] They knew God, but they did not give glory to God or thank him. Their thinking became useless. Their foolish minds were filled with darkness. [22] They said they were wise, but they became fools. [23] They traded the glory of God who lives forever for the worship of idols

made to look like earthly people, birds, animals, and snakes.

²⁴ Because they did these things, God left them and let them go their sinful way, wanting only to do evil. As a result, they became full of sexual sin, using their bodies wrongly with each other. ²⁵ They traded the truth of God for a lie. They worshiped and served what had been created instead of the God who created those things, who should be praised forever. Amen.

Romans 1:21-25

7. What images or things do people in our society worship?

_____

_____

_____

_____

_____

_____

_____

8. Explain how people trade God's truth for a lie.

_____

_____

_____

_____

_____

_____

_____

9. How would our world be different if we consistently worshipped our Creator rather than the created?

_____

_____

_____

_____

_____

_____

_____

My Reflections

"Who has more reason to worship than the astronomer who has seen the stars? Than the surgeon who has held a heart? Than the oceanographer who has pondered the depths? The more we know, the more we should be amazed."—Max

Journal

What is most amazing about God's presence in my world and in my life?

18

For Further Study

To learn more about worshipping God as the Creator, read Psalm 100:1-3; Psalm 104:1-24; Psalm 148:1-14; Amos 4:13.

Additional Questions

10. In what ways does our society care for nature more than the God who created it?

_____

_____

_____

_____

_____

11. What evidence of idolatry do you see around you?

_____

_____

_____

_____

_____

12. What practical steps can we take to resist the sin of idolatry?

_____

_____

_____

_____

_____

Additional Thoughts

_____

_____

_____

_____

_____

_____

_____

_____

_____

_____

Too Good to Be True?

"God's highest dream is not to make us rich, not to make us successful or popular or famous. God's dream is to make us right with him."

—Max Lucado

21

1. Think of someone who has sacrificed to make a dream come true. What did that person give up to achieve his or her goal?

_____

_____

_____

_____

_____

_____

_____

A Moment with Max

The perfect record of Jesus was given to you, and your imperfect record was given to Christ. Jesus was "not guilty, but he suffered for those who are guilty to bring you to God" (1 Peter 3:18). As a result, God's holiness is honored and his children are forgiven.

By his perfect life Jesus fulfilled the commands of the law. By his death he satisfied the demands of sin. Jesus suffered not like a sinner, but as a sinner. Why else would he cry, "My God, my God, why have You forsaken Me" (Matthew 27:46 NKJV)?

Ponder the achievement of God. He doesn't condone our sin; nor does he compromise his standard. He doesn't ignore our rebellion; nor does he relax his demands. Rather than dismiss our sin he assumes our sin and, incredibly, sentences himself. God's holiness is honored. Our sin is punished. And we are redeemed. God is still God. The wages of sin is still death. And we are made perfect. . . . God does what we cannot do so we can be what we dare not dream, perfect before God. He justly justifies the unjust.

22

2. How would you feel if someone offered to pay a debt for you (a college loan or credit card bill)?

_____

_____

_____

_____

3. What sometimes hinders us from fully accepting God's gift of forgiveness?

_____

_____

_____

_____

A Message from the Word

[21] But God has a way to make people right with him without the law, and he has now shown us that way which the law and the prophets told us about. [22] God makes people right with himself through their faith in Jesus Christ. This is true for all who believe in Christ, because all people are the same: [23] All have sinned and are not good enough for God's glory, [24] and all need to be made right with God by his grace, which is a free gift. They need to be made free from sin through Jesus Christ. [25] God gave him as a way to forgive sin through faith in the blood of Jesus' death. This showed that God always does what is right and fair, as in the past when he was patient and did not punish people for their sins.

Romans 3:21-25

[17] If anyone belongs to Christ, there is a new creation. The old things have gone; everything is made new! [18] All this is from God. Through Christ, God made peace between us and himself, and God gave us the work of telling everyone about the peace we can have with him. [19] God was in Christ, making peace between the world and himself. In Christ, God did not hold the world guilty of its sins. And he gave us this message of peace. [20] So we have been sent to speak for Christ. It is as if God is calling to you through us. We speak for Christ when we beg you to be at peace with God. [21] Christ had no sin, but God made him become sin so that in Christ we could become right with God.

2 Corinthians 5:17-21

4. What similarities do you see between reconciling one's relationship with God and reconciling a financial statement?

_____

_____

_____

_____

5. What does God want in return for the price Christ paid?

_____

_____

_____

_____

_____

6. How should Christ's sacrifice for us affect our everyday interactions with others?

_____

_____

_____

_____

_____

24

More from the Word

[16] Because he was full of grace and truth, from him we all received one gift after another. [17] The law was given through Moses, but grace and truth came through Jesus Christ.

John 1:16–17

[18] Christ himself suffered for sins once. He was not guilty, but he suffered for those who are guilty to bring you to God. His body was killed, but he was made alive in the spirit.

1 Peter 3:18

7. For what has God forgiven you?

_____

_____

_____

_____

8. How does grace and truth come through Jesus Christ?

_____

_____

_____ 25

_____

9. If Christ died, the righteous for the unrighteous, why do we so often try to "clean up our act" before accepting God's grace?

_____

_____

_____

_____

My Reflections

"We have attempted to reach the moon but scarcely made it off the ground. We tried to swim the Atlantic, but couldn't get beyond the reef. We have attempted to scale the Everest of salvation, but we have yet to leave the base camp, much less ascend the slope. The quest is simply too great; we don't need more supplies or muscle or technique; we need a helicopter.

"Can't you hear it hovering?

"'God has a way to make people right with him' (Romans 3:21). How vital that we embrace this truth."—Max

Journal

In what new way can I embrace the fact that Christ sacrificed himself to have a relationship with me?

_____

_____

_____

_____

_____

_____

_____

_____

_____

_____

27

For Further Study

To learn more about Christ's sacrificial death, read Mark 15:33–39; Romans 5:15–17; Galatians 2:19–21; Hebrews 2:9.

Additional Questions

10. How would you explain to a friend why Jesus had to sacrifice his life to make us right with God?

_____

_____

_____

_____

_____

11. Why do some people try to earn God's favor instead of accept his forgiveness?

_____

_____

_____

_____

_____

12. How does Christ's death make us righteous?

_____

_____

_____

_____

_____

Additional Thoughts

_____

_____

_____

_____

_____

_____

_____

_____

_____

_____

Unlimited Line of Credit

"How do I deal with the debt I owe to God?
Deny it? My conscience won't let me.
Find worse sins in others? God won't fall for that....
Try to pay it off? I could, but that takes us back to
the problem. We don't know the cost of sin. We don't
even know how much we owe."—Max Lucado

31

1. In your own words, describe the debt you owe to God.

_____

_____

_____

_____

_____

_____

A Moment with Max

Simply put: The cost of your sins is more than you can pay. The gift of your God is more than you can imagine. "A person is made right with God through faith," Paul explains, "not through obeying the law" (Romans 3:28).

This may very well be the most difficult spiritual truth for us to embrace. For some reason, people accept Jesus as Lord before they accept him as Savior. It's easier to comprehend his power than his mercy. We'll celebrate the empty tomb long before we'll kneel at the cross. We, like Thomas, could die for Christ before we'd let Christ die for us.

We aren't alone. We aren't the first to struggle with Paul's presentation of grace. Apparently, the first ones to doubt the epistle to the Romans were the first to read it. In fact, you get the impression Paul can hear their questions. The apostle lifts his pen from the page and imagines his readers: some squirming, some doubting, some denying. Anticipating their thoughts, he deals with their objections.

2. Why must it be easier to comprehend God's power than his mercy?

32

_____

_____

_____

_____

3. How do you feel about the fact that you cannot be "good enough" in your own power to remain right with God?

_____

_____

_____

_____

A Message from the Word

27 So do we have a reason to brag about ourselves? No! And why not? It is the way of faith that stops all bragging, not the way of trying to obey the law. 28 A person is made right with God through faith, not through obeying the law. 29 Is God only the God of the Jews? Is he not also the God of those who are not Jews? 30 Of course he is, because there is only one God. He will make Jews right with him by their faith, and he will also make those who are not Jews right with him through their faith. 31 So do we destroy the law by following the way of faith? No! Faith causes us to be what the law truly wants.

1 So what can we say that Abraham, the father of our people, learned about faith? 2 If Abraham was made right by the things he did, he had a reason to brag. But this is not God's view, 3 because the Scripture says, "Abraham believed God, and God accepted Abraham's faith, and that faith made him right with God."

4 When people work, their pay is not given as a gift, but as something earned. 5 But people cannot do any work that will make them right with God. So they must trust in him, who makes even evil people right in his sight. Then God accepts their faith, and that makes them right with him. 6 David said the same thing. He said that people are truly blessed when God, without paying attention to good deeds, makes people right with himself.

7 "Happy are they
    whose sins are forgiven,
    whose wrongs are pardoned.
8 Happy is the person
    whom the Lord does not consider guilty."

Romans 3:27—4:8

4. Describe Abraham's faith.

_____

_____

_____

_____

5. Why is it difficult for some people to believe that they can be justified through faith alone?

_____

_____

_____

_____

6. If our faith is credited to us as righteousness, why do we obey God's laws?

_____

_____

_____

_____

_____

More from the Word

[18] There was no hope that Abraham would have children. But Abraham believed God and continued hoping, and so he became the father of many nations. As God told him, "Your descendants also will be too many to count." [19] Abraham was almost a hundred years old, much past the age for having children, and Sarah could not have children. Abraham thought about all this, but his faith in God did not become weak. [20] He never doubted that God would keep his promise, and he never stopped believing. He grew stronger in his faith and gave praise to God. [21] Abraham felt sure that God was able to do what he had

promised. [22] So, "God accepted Abraham's faith, and that faith made him right with God." [23] Those words ("God accepted Abraham's faith") were written not only for Abraham [24] but also for us. God will accept us also because we believe in the One who raised Jesus our Lord from the dead. [25] Jesus was given to die for our sins, and he was raised from the dead to make us right with God.

Romans 4:18-25

7. What is the role of faith in salvation?

_____

_____

_____

_____

8. What experiences in your life have strengthened your faith?

_____

_____

_____

_____

9. Is faith or obedience more important to God? Why?

_____

_____

_____

_____

My Reflections

"There's not a one of us who must remain in debt. The same God who gave a child to Abraham has promised grace to us.

"What's more incredible, Sarah telling Abraham that he was a daddy, or God calling you and me righteous? Both are absurd. Both are too good to be true. But both are from God."—Max

Journal

In what area of my life do I need to accept God's grace through faith?

_____

_____

_____

_____

_____

_____

_____

_____

_____

_____

_____

_____

For Further Study

To study more about faith in God, read Matthew 8:23-27; Mark 9:17-27; Galatians 5:4-6; Colossians 2:9-12.

Additional Questions

10. Describe a time when you, like Abraham, were asked to believe something that seemed impossible.

_____

_____

_____

_____

_____

11. How does God test our faith? Why?

_____

_____

_____

_____

_____

12. In what practical ways can we prepare ourselves for times of testing?

_____

_____

_____

_____

_____

Additional Thoughts

_____

_____

_____

_____

_____

_____

_____

_____

_____

_____

Backstage Pass

"If the first four chapters of Romans tell us anything, they tell us we are living a life we don't deserve."—Max Lucado

1. Describe a time when you received something you didn't think you deserved. How did you feel?

_____

_____

_____

_____

_____

_____

A Moment with Max

Max shares these insights with us in his book *In the Grip of Grace*.

Christ meets you outside the throne room, takes you by the hand, and walks you into the presence of God. Upon entrance we find grace, not condemnation; mercy, not punishment. Where we would never be granted an audience with the king, we are now welcomed into his presence.

If you are a parent you understand this. If a child you don't know appears on your doorstep and asks to spend the night, what would you do? Likely you would ask him his name, where he lives, find out why he is roaming the streets, and contact his parents. On the other hand, if a youngster enters your house escorted by your child, that child is welcome. The same is true with God. By becoming friends with the Son we gain access to the Father.

Jesus promised, "All who stand before others and say they believe in me, I will say before my Father in heaven that they belong to me" (Matthew 10:32). Because we are friends of his Son, we have entrance to the throne room. He ushers us into that "blessing of God's grace that we now enjoy" (Romans 5:2).

42

2. Think of a time when someone has vouched for you. What did you feel you owed that person?

_____

_____

_____

_____

3. How has Christ's action on your behalf impacted your life?

_____

_____

_____

_____

A Message from the Word

¹ Since we have been made right with God by our faith, we have peace with God. This happened through our Lord Jesus Christ, ² who has brought us into that blessing of God's grace that we now enjoy. And we are happy because of the hope we have of sharing God's glory. ³ We also have joy with our troubles, because we know that these troubles produce patience. ⁴ And patience produces character, and character produces hope. ⁵ And this hope will never disappoint us, because God has poured out his love to fill our hearts. He gave us his love through the Holy Spirit, whom God has given to us.

⁶ When we were unable to help ourselves, at the moment of our need, Christ died for us, although we were living against God. ⁷ Very few people will die to save the life of someone else. Although perhaps for a good person someone might possibly die. ⁸ But God shows his great love for us in this way: Christ died for us while we were still sinners.

⁹ So through Christ we will surely be saved from God's anger, because we have been made right with God by the blood of Christ's death. ¹⁰ While we were God's enemies, he made friends with us through the death of his Son. Surely, now that we are his friends, he will save us through his Son's life. ¹¹ And not only that, but now we are also very happy in God through our Lord Jesus Christ. Through him we are now God's friends again.

Romans 5:1–11

43

4. How did God tangibly demonstrate his love for us?

_____

_____

_____

_____

5. How would you describe to a friend the way to find peace with God?

_____

_____

_____

_____

6. How does strength of character produce hope in us?

_____

_____

_____

_____

More from the Word

[13] But now in Christ Jesus, you who were far away from God are brought near through the blood of Christ's death. [14] Christ himself is our peace. He made both Jewish people and those who are not Jews one people. They were separated as if there were a wall between them, but Christ broke down that wall of hate by giving his own body. [15] The Jewish law had many commands and rules, but Christ ended that law. His purpose was to make the two groups of people become one new people in him and in this way make peace. [16] It was also Christ's purpose to end the hatred between the two groups, to make them into one body, and to bring them back to God. Christ did all this with his death on the cross. [17] Christ came and preached peace to you who were far away from God, and to those who were near to God. [18] Yes, it is through Christ we all have the right to come to the Father in one Spirit.

[19] Now you who are not Jewish are not foreigners or strangers any longer, but are citizens together with God's holy people. You belong to

God's family. [20] You are like a building that was built on the foundation of the apostles and prophets. Christ Jesus himself is the most important stone in that building, [21] and that whole building is joined together in Christ. He makes it grow and become a holy temple in the Lord. [22] And in Christ you, too, are being built together with the Jews into a place where God lives through the Spirit.

Ephesians 2:13-22

7. What does it mean to be the dwelling place of the Spirit of God?

_____

_____

_____

_____

8. If we have access to God, what keeps us from interacting with him?

_____

_____

_____

_____

9. How does our citizenship in heaven affect our life on earth?

_____

_____

_____

_____

My Reflections

"Grace delivered us from fear, but watch how quickly we return. Grace told us we didn't have to spend our lives looking over our shoulders, but look at us glancing backward.... Don't we know better?"—Max

Journal

If I were face to face with God, physically before his throne, how would I tell him what his grace means to me?

_____

_____

_____

_____

_____

_____

_____

_____

_____

_____

_____

_____

For Further Study

To learn more about our access to God, read John 14:6; Colossians 1:9–14; 1 John 2:1–3.

Additional Questions

10. What causes people to ignore God's grace?

_____

_____

_____

_____

_____

_____

11. List some things that keep you from enjoying God's presence.

_____

_____

_____

_____

_____

_____

12. What concrete action can you take to draw closer to God?

_____

_____

_____

_____

_____

Additional Thoughts

_____

_____

_____

_____

_____

_____

_____

_____

_____

_____

Certificate of Adoption

"It is not our offerings that grant us a place at the feast; indeed, anything we bring appears puny at his table. Our admission of hunger is the only demand ...."—Max Lucado

51

1. Why is it difficult for most people to admit they are in need of something?

_____

_____

_____

_____

_____

_____

_____

A Moment with Max

Mephibosheth was the son of Jonathan, the grandson of Saul, who was the first king of Israel. Saul and Jonathan were killed in battle, leaving the throne to be occupied by David. In those days the new king often staked out his territory by exterminating the family of the previous king.

David had no intention of following this tradition, but the family of Saul didn't know that. So they hurried to escape. Of special concern to them was five-year-old Mephibosheth, for upon the deaths of his father and uncle, he was the presumptive heir to the throne. If David was intent on murdering Saul's heirs, this boy would be first on his list. So the family got out of Dodge. But in the haste of the moment, Mephibosheth slipped from the arms of his nurse, permanently damaging both feet. For the rest of his life he would be a cripple.

If his story is beginning to sound familiar, it should. You and he have a lot in common. Weren't you also born of royalty? And don't you carry the wounds of a fall? And hasn't each of us lived in fear of a king we have never seen?

2. David eventually brought Mephibosheth, the crippled son of his enemy, into the palace to eat at the royal table. From your experience, how does this mirror the way God has treated you?

_____

_____

_____

_____

_____

3. Mephibosheth's brokenness was physical. What kinds of brokenness do you see around you that require God's grace?

_____

_____

_____

_____

_____

A Message from the Word

[12] So, my brothers and sisters, we must not be ruled by our sinful selves or live the way our sinful selves want. [13] If you use your lives to do the wrong things your sinful selves want, you will die spiritually. But if you use the Spirit's help to stop doing the wrong things you do with your body, you will have true life.

[14] The true children of God are those who let God's Spirit lead them.

Romans 8:12-14

53

[1] The Father has loved us so much that we are called children of God. And we really are his children. The reason the people in the world do not know us is that they have not known him. [2] Dear friends, now we are children of God, and we have not yet been shown what we will be in the future. But we know that when Christ comes again, we will be like him, because we will see him as he really is.

1 John 3:1-2

4. How have you personally experienced the lavish love of the Father?

_____

_____

_____

_____

5. Why do you think God continues to love and redeem us when he could give up and start over?

_____

_____

_____

_____

_____

6. List some ways believers are led by the Spirit of God.

_____

_____

_____

_____

_____

More from the Word

⁴ But when the kindness and love of God our Savior was shown, ⁵ he saved us because of his mercy. It was not because of good deeds we did to be right with him. He saved us through the washing that made us new people through the Holy Spirit. ⁶ God poured out richly upon us that Holy Spirit through Jesus Christ our Savior. ⁷ Being made right with God by his grace, we could have the hope of receiving the life that never ends.

⁸ This teaching is true, and I want you to be sure the people understand these things. Then those who believe in God will be careful to use their lives for doing good. These things are good and will help everyone.

Titus 3:4-8

⁹ He will not always accuse us,
    and he will not be angry forever.
¹⁰ He has not punished us as our sins should be punished;
    he has not repaid us for the evil we have done.
¹¹ As high as the sky is above the earth,
    so great is his love for those who respect him.
¹² He has taken our sins away from us
    as far as the east is from west.
¹³ The Lord has mercy on those who respect him,
    as a father has mercy on his children.
¹⁴ He knows how we were made;
    he remembers that we are dust.

Psalm 103:9-14

7. On whom does the Lord have compassion?

_____

_____

_____

_____

_____

8. What evidence of God's mercy do you see in your life?

_____

_____

_____

_____

_____

9. List some ways we can show to others the kindness God has shown to us.

_____

_____

_____

_____

_____

_____

My Reflections

"Children of royalty, crippled by the fall, permanently marred by sin. Living parenthetical lives in the chronicles of earth only to be remembered by the king. Driven not by our beauty but by his promise, he calls us to himself and invites us to take a permanent place at his table. Though we often limp more than we walk, we take our place next to the other sinners-made-saints and we share in God's glory."—Max

Journal

In what broken part of my life do I need to seek God's grace and healing?

_____

_____

_____

_____

_____

_____

_____

_____

_____

_____

_____

_____

_____

_____

For Further Study

To learn more about being a child of God, read John 1:9-13; Ephesians 1:3-10; 1 John 5:1-5.

Additional Questions

10. Describe how you become a child of God.

_____

_____

_____

_____

_____

11. How does being a child of God, saved by his grace, change the way we look at the world?

_____

_____

_____

_____

_____

12. In what circumstances do you need to remind yourself that you belong to God?

_____

_____

_____

_____

_____

Additional Thoughts

_____

_____

_____

_____

_____

_____

_____

_____

Everyday Grace

"Where the grace of God is missed, bitterness is born. But where the grace of God is embraced, forgiveness flourishes. . . . The more we immerse ourselves in grace, the more likely we are to give grace." —Max Lucado

1. What is the best method you have found for quitting bad habits and developing good habits?

_____

_____

_____

_____

_____

_____

_____

A Moment with Max

Max shares these insights with us in his book *In the Grip of Grace*.

Before Christ our lives were out of control, sloppy, and indulgent. We didn't even know we were slobs until we met him.

Then he moved in. Things began to change. What we threw around we began putting away. What we neglected we cleaned up. What had been clutter became order. Oh, there were and still are occasional lapses of thought and deed, but by and large he got our house in order.

Suddenly we find ourselves wanting to do good. Go back to the old mess? Are you kidding? "In the past you were slaves to sin—sin controlled you. But thank God, you fully obeyed the things that you were taught. You were made free from sin, and now you are slaves to goodness" (Romans 6:17–18).

2. What is one godly habit you are working to incorporate into your daily routine?

_____

_____

_____

_____

_____

3. List some habits we could all develop that would help us live within the grip of God's grace.

_____

_____

_____

_____

_____

A Message from the Word

[11] That is the way we should live, because God's grace that can save everyone has come. [12] It teaches us not to live against God nor to do the evil things the world wants to do. Instead, that grace teaches us to live now in a wise and right way and in a way that shows we serve God. [13] We should live like that while we wait for our great hope and the coming of the glory of our great God and Savior Jesus Christ. [14] He gave himself for us so he might pay the price to free us from all evil and to make us pure people who belong only to him—people who are always wanting to do good deeds.

Titus 2:11-14

[8] Brothers and sisters, think about the things that are good and worthy of praise. Think about the things that are true and honorable and right and pure and beautiful and respected. [9] Do what you learned and received from me, what I told you, and what you saw me do. And the God who gives peace will be with you.

Philippians 4:8-9

63

4. List some things that are good, true, pure, and/or beautiful?

_____

_____

_____

_____

_____

_____

_____

5. What steps can we take to begin eliminating habitual sin from our lives?

_____

_____

_____

_____

_____

6. Think of someone you believe has learned to live habitually within God's grace. Describe that person's lifestyle.

_____

_____

_____

_____

_____

More from the Word

[15] So what should we do? Should we sin because we are under grace and not under law? No! [16] Surely you know that when you give yourselves like slaves to obey someone, then you are really slaves of that person. The person you obey is your master. You can follow sin, which brings spiritual death, or you can obey God, which makes you right with him. [17] In the past you were slaves to sin—sin controlled you. But thank God, you fully obeyed the things that you were taught. [18] You were made free from sin, and now you are slaves to goodness.

Romans 6:15-18

7. Describe what it means to be set free from sin and become a slave to righteousness.

_____

_____

_____

_____

_____

8. How does grace fit in with our efforts to obey God's law?

_____

_____

_____

_____

9. List some of the joys and rewards of obedience you have experienced.

_____

_____

_____

_____

My Reflections

"How can we who have been made right not live righteous lives? How can we who have been loved not love? How can we who have been blessed not bless? How can we who have been given grace not live graciously?

"Paul seems stunned that an alternative would even exist! How could grace result in anything but gracious living?"—Max

Journal

Who is one person I have not treated graciously in the past? How can I extend God's grace to that person today?

_____

_____

_____

_____

_____

_____

_____

_____

_____

_____

_____

For Further Study

To learn more about living graciously, read Proverbs 22:11; Matthew 6:14-15; 1 Corinthians 1:4-9; Colossians 4:2-6.

Additional Questions

10. In what ways does living in God's grace affect the way you pray?

_____

_____

_____

_____

_____

_____

11. List some ways we take God's grace for granted.

_____

_____

_____

_____

_____

12. How would your family life be different if you consistently lived graciously in your home?

_____

_____

_____

_____

_____

_____

Additional Thoughts

_____ 69

_____

_____

_____

_____

_____

_____

_____

_____

_____

_____

Turning Yourself In

*"**P**erhaps we didn't take money but we've taken advantage or taken control or taken leave of our senses and then, like the thief, we've taken off. Dashing down alleys of deceit. Hiding behind buildings of work to be done or deadlines to be met. Though we try to act normal, anyone who looks closely at us can see we are on the lam: Eyes darting and hands fidgeting, we chatter nervously committed to the cover-up, we scheme and squirm, changing the topic and changing direction. We don't want anyone to know the truth, especially God."* —Max Lucado

1. Think of a time when you felt very guilty about something. How did your guilty conscience affect your behavior?

_____

_____

_____

A Moment with Max

Max shares these insights with us in his book *In the Grip of Grace.*

Confession does for the soul what preparing the land does for the field. Before the farmer sows the seed he works the acreage, removing the rocks and pulling the stumps. He knows that seed grows better if the land is prepared. Confession is the act of inviting God to walk the acreage of our hearts. "There is a rock of greed over here, Father; I can't budge it. And that tree of guilt near the fence? Its roots are long and deep. And may I show you some dry soil, too crusty for seed?" God's seed grows better if the soil of the heart is cleared.

And so the Father and the Son walk the field together; digging and pulling, preparing the heart for fruit. Confession invites the Father to work the soil of the soul.

2. If God knows us better than we know ourselves and is eager to forgive us, what keeps us from confessing our sin to him?

_____

_____

_____

_____

3. Describe the freedom that confession brings.

_____

_____

_____

_____

_____

A Message from the Word

[13] Anyone who is having troubles should pray. Anyone who is happy should sing praises. [14] Anyone who is sick should call the church's elders. They should pray for and pour oil on the person in the name of the Lord. [15] And the prayer that is said with faith will make the sick person well; the Lord will heal that person. And if the person has sinned, the sins will be forgiven. [16] Confess your sins to each other and pray for each other so God can heal you. When a believing person prays, great things happen.

James 5:13-16

[8] If we say we have no sin, we are fooling ourselves, and the truth is not in us. [9] But if we confess our sins, he will forgive our sins, because we can trust God to do what is right. He will cleanse us from all the wrongs we have done. [10] If we say we have not sinned, we make God a liar, and we do not accept God's teaching.

1 John 1:8-10

73

4. Why is it so difficult to confess our sins to one another?

_____

_____

_____

_____

5. What criteria do most people follow to determine which sins to openly confess to others?

_____

_____

_____

_____

6. In what circumstances do you think it is wise to admit your mistakes to a spouse or friend?

_____

_____

_____

_____

_____

More from the Word

[3] When I kept things to myself,
     I felt weak deep inside me.
     I moaned all day long.
[4] Day and night you punished me.
     My strength was gone as in the summer heat.
[5] Then I confessed my sins to you
     and didn't hide my guilt.
I said, "I will confess my sins to the Lord,"
     and you forgave my guilt.

Psalm 32:3-5

7. How does chronic guilt affect us physically?

_____

_____

_____

_____

_____

8. How do we relate to God and other people differently when we have confessed and received forgiveness?

_____

_____

_____

_____

9. How can we nurture an atmosphere of openness and honesty in our churches and communities?

_____

_____

_____

_____

My Reflections

"Am I missing the mark when I say that many of us attend church on the run? Am I out of line when I say many of us spend life on the run?

"Am I overstating the case when I announce, "Grace means you don't have to run anymore!" It's the truth. Grace means it's finally safe to turn ourselves in." —Max

Journal

How can I practice confession on a more regular basis?

For Further Study

To learn more about confession, read Numbers 5:5-7; Psalm 38:18; Proverbs 28:13.

Additional Questions

10. Why do people say, "Admitting your problem is the first step to overcoming it"?

_____

_____

_____

_____

_____

11. Think of the most difficult confession you've ever made. What did you learn from that experience?

_____

_____

_____

_____

_____

_____

12. How can you make it easier for your family members and friends to confess their mistakes to you?

_____

_____

_____

_____

_____

_____

Additional Thoughts

_____

_____

_____

_____

_____

_____

_____

_____

_____

_____

_____

_____

Enough Is Enough!

"Is God still a good God when he says no?"

—*Max Lucado*

1. Describe a time when you prayed for something and didn't receive it.

_____

_____

_____

_____

_____

_____

A Moment with Max

Max shares these insights with us in his book *In the Grip of Grace*.

There are times when the one thing you want is the one thing you never get. You're not being picky or demanding; you're only obeying his command to "ask God for everything you need" (Philippians 4:6). All you want is an open door or an extra day or an answered prayer, for which you will be thankful.

And so you pray and wait.

No answer.

You pray and wait.

No answer.

You pray and wait.

May I ask a very important question? What if God says no?

What if the request is delayed or even denied? When God says no to you, how will you respond? If God says, "I've given you my grace, and that is enough," will you be content?

2. For what reasons do you think God sometimes says no to our prayers?

82

_____

_____

_____

_____

_____

3. How do you console yourself when you earnestly pray for something and God withholds it from you?

_____

_____

_____

_____

A Message from the Word

[7] So that I would not become too proud of the wonderful things that were shown to me, a painful physical problem was given to me. This problem was a messenger from Satan, sent to beat me and keep me from being too proud. [8] I begged the Lord three times to take this problem away from me. [9] But he said to me, "My grace is enough for you. When you are weak, my power is made perfect in you." So I am very happy to brag about my weaknesses. Then Christ's power can live in me. [10] For this reason I am happy when I have weaknesses, insults, hard times, sufferings, and all kinds of troubles for Christ. Because when I am weak, then I am truly strong.

2 Corinthians 12:7-10

4. Why does God sometimes says no when we ask him to remove difficult elements from our lives?

_____

_____

_____

_____

_____

5. How has God's grace helped you deal with the "thorns in your flesh"?

_____

_____

_____

_____

6. List some reasons why we should continue to pray even when it seems God isn't responding.

_____

_____

_____

_____

_____

More from the Word

¹⁵ For our high priest is able to understand our weaknesses. When he lived on earth, he was tempted in every way that we are, but he did not sin. ¹⁶ Let us, then, feel very sure that we can come before God's throne where there is grace. There we can receive mercy and grace to help us when we need it.

Hebrews 4:15–16

7. In what ways does Christ's experience on earth give us confidence?

_____

_____

_____

_____

_____

8. How did Jesus accept God's will in his own life on earth? Describe how we can follow his example.

_____

_____

_____

_____

_____

_____

9. How can God's grace comfort us in times of hardship and disappointment?

_____

_____

_____

_____

_____

My Reflections

"You wonder why God doesn't remove temptation from your life? If he did, you might lean on your strength instead of his grace. A few stumbles might be what you need to convince you: His grace is sufficient for your sin." —Max

Journal

What lessons can I learn from a current difficulty in my life?

_____

_____

_____

_____

_____

_____

_____

_____

_____

_____

_____

_____

_____

_____

For Further Study

To learn more about finding God's grace through prayer, read Proverbs 15:29; Matthew 21:21-22; Philippians 4:6; James 5:16.

Additional Questions

10. Describe a time when God answered one of your prayers in an unexpected way.

_____

_____

_____

_____

_____

11. Why is it difficult for some people to believe that God's grace is enough to get them through the hard times?

_____

_____

_____

_____

12. How can you depend more fully on God to help you through the difficulties you face this week?

_____

_____

_____

_____

_____

Additional Thoughts

_____

_____

_____

_____

_____

_____

_____

_____

_____

_____

Civil Unrest

"Before I knew the law, I was at peace. Now that I know the law, an insurrection has occurred. I'm a torn man. On one hand I know what to do, but I don't want to do it."

—Max Lucado   91

1. Think of a recent internal struggle. Which of these battles would you compare it to: the Civil War, World War II, American Gladiators, or Family Feud? Why?

_____

_____

_____

_____

_____

_____

_____

A Moment with Max

Max shares these insights with us in his book *In the Grip of Grace.*

Your temptation isn't late-breaking news in heaven. Your sin doesn't surprise God. He saw it coming. Is there any reason to think that the One who received you the first time won't receive you every time?

Besides the very fact that you are under attack must mean that you're on the right side. Did you notice who else had times of struggle? Paul did.... He is not describing a struggle of the past, but a struggle in the present. For all we know, Paul was engaged in spiritual combat even as he wrote this letter. You mean the apostle Paul battled sin while he was writing a book in the Bible? Can you think of a more strategic time for Satan to attack? Is it possible that Satan feared the fruit of this epistle to the Romans?

Could it be that he fears the fruits of your life?

2. What does it feel like to be under spiritual attack when you are trying to do the right thing?

_____

_____

_____

_____

_____

3. If you think it's possible, list some ways we can sin without even being aware of it.

_____

_____

_____

_____

A Message from the Word

⁷ You might think I am saying that sin and the law are the same thing. That is not true. But the law was the only way I could learn what sin meant. I would never have known what it means to want to take something belonging to someone else if the law had not said, "You must not want to take your neighbor's things." ⁸ And sin found a way to use that command and cause me to want all kinds of things I should not want. But without the law, sin has no power. ⁹ I was alive before I knew the law. But when the law's command came to me, then sin began to live, ¹⁰ and I died. The command was meant to bring life, but for me it brought death. ¹¹ Sin found a way to fool me by using the command to make me die.

¹² So the law is holy, and the command is holy and right and good. ¹³ Does this mean that something that is good brought death to me? No! Sin used something that is good to bring death to me. This happened so that I could see what sin is really like; the command was used to show that sin is very evil.

¹⁴ We know that the law is spiritual, but I am not spiritual since sin rules me as if I were its slave. ¹⁵ I do not understand the things I do. I do not do what I want to do, and I do the things I hate. ¹⁶ And if I do not want to do the hated things I do, that means I agree that the law is good. ¹⁷ But I am not really the one who is doing these hated things; it is sin living in me that does them. ¹⁸ Yes, I know that nothing good lives in me—I mean nothing good lives in the part of me that is earthly and sinful. I want to do the things that are good, but I do not do them. ¹⁹ I do not do the good things I want to do, but I do the bad things I do not want to do. ²⁰ So if I do things I do not want to do, then I am not the one doing them. It is sin living in me that does those things.

Romans 7:7-20

⁹³

4. Think of someone who seems to resist temptation consistently. What can you learn from that person about overcoming sin?

_____

_____

_____

_____

5. What weapons are available to us in our battle against sin?

_____

_____

_____

_____

6. What do you think prevents us from using these weapons effectively?

_____

_____

_____

_____

More from the Word

[15] The Spirit we received does not make us slaves again to fear; it makes us children of God. With that Spirit we cry out, "Father." [16] And the Spirit himself joins with our spirits to say we are God's children. [17] If we are God's children, we will receive blessings from God together with Christ. But we must suffer as Christ suffered so that we will have glory as Christ has glory.

Romans 8:15–17

[16] So I tell you: Live by following the Spirit. Then you will not do what your sinful selves want. [17] Our sinful selves want what is against the Spirit, and the Spirit wants what is against our sinful selves. The two are against each other, so you cannot do just what you please. [18] But if the Spirit is leading you, you are not under the law.

Galatians 5:16–18

7. In what ways can we discern and follow the Spirit's leading?

_____

_____

_____

_____

8. What does it mean for us to share in Christ's suffering and glory?

_____

_____

_____

_____

_____

_____

9. If we are heirs with Christ, what is our inheritance?

_____

_____

_____

_____

_____

My Reflections

"When you came to Christ did he know every sin you'd committed up until that point? Yes. Did Christ know every sin you would commit in the future? Yes, he knew that too. So Jesus saved you, knowing all the sins you would ever commit until the end of your life? Yes. You mean he is willing to call you his child even though he knows each and every mistake of your past and future? Yes."—Max

Journal

How can I express my thanks to Christ for his unconditional love?

_____

_____

_____

_____

_____

_____

_____

_____

_____

_____

For Further Study

To learn more about our battle with sin, read Ephesians 6:10–18;
1 Corinthians 10:13; 2 Corinthians 10:1–6; 1 Timothy 6:11–16; James
4:1–3.

Additional Questions

10. How does God's spirit help us overcome sin?

_____

_____

_____

_____

_____

_____

11. When has God provided a way for you to escape temptation and
sin?

_____

_____

_____

_____

_____

12. How can prayer help you in your battle against sin?

_____

_____

_____

_____

Additional Thoughts

_____

_____

_____

_____

_____

_____

_____

_____

_____

_____

One Good Turn Deserves . . .

"Grace makes three proclamations.
First, only God can forgive my godlessness....
Second, only God can judge my neighbor....
Third, I must accept who God accepts....
Easier said than done."—Max Lucado

1. What are some traits in others that make it difficult for you to accept them?

_____

_____

_____

_____

_____

_____

_____

A Moment with Max

Max shares these insights with us in his book *In the Grip of Grace*.

God has enlisted us in his navy and placed us on his ship. The boat has one purpose—to carry us safely to the other shore.

This is no cruise ship; it's a battleship. We aren't called to a life of leisure; we are called to a life of service. Each of us has a different task. Some, concerned with those who are drowning, are snatching people from the water. Others are occupied with the enemy, so they man the cannons of prayer and worship. Still others devote themselves to the crew, feeding and training the crew members.

Though different, we are the same. Each can tell of a personal encounter with the captain, for each has received a personal call. He found us among the shanties of the seaport and invited us to follow him. . . .

Though the battle is fierce, the boat is safe, for our captain is God. The ship will not sink. For that, there is no concern.

There is concern, however, regarding the disharmony of the crew.

2. List some things that cause tension and disharmony among Christians.

_____

_____

_____

_____

3. How has your personal encounter with God changed the way you relate to others?

_____

_____

_____

_____

A Message from the Word

[5] Patience and encouragement come from God. And I pray that God will help you all agree with each other the way Christ Jesus wants. [6] Then you will all be joined together, and you will give glory to God the Father of our Lord Jesus Christ. [7] Christ accepted you, so you should accept each other, which will bring glory to God.

Romans 15:5-7

[2] Always be humble, gentle, and patient, accepting each other in love. [3] You are joined together with peace through the Spirit, so make every effort to continue together in this way. [4] There is one body and one Spirit, and God called you to have one hope. [5] There is one Lord, one faith, and one baptism. [6] There is one God and Father of everything. He rules everything and is everywhere and is in everything.

[31] Do not be bitter or angry or mad. Never shout angrily or say things to hurt others. Never do anything evil. [32] Be kind and loving to each other, and forgive each other just as God forgave you in Christ.

Ephesians 4:2-6, 31-32

103

4. What kinds of disagreements cause people to give up on their relationships?

_____

_____

_____

_____

_____

5. Describe in practical terms what it means for Christians to live in unity.

_____

_____

_____

_____

_____

6. List some practical steps we can take to get along with one another.

_____

_____

_____

_____

More from the Word

[9] Your love must be real. Hate what is evil, and hold on to what is good. [10] Love each other like brothers and sisters. Give each other more honor than you want for yourselves. [11] Do not be lazy but work hard, serving the Lord with all your heart. [12] Be joyful because you have hope. Be patient when trouble comes, and pray at all times. [13] Share with God's people who need help. Bring strangers in need into your homes.

Romans 12:9-13

[8] Do not owe people anything, except always owe love to each other, because the person who loves others has obeyed all the law. [9] The law says, "You must not be guilty of adultery. You must not murder anyone. You must not steal. You must not want to take your neighbor's things." All these commands and all others are really only one rule: "Love your neighbor as you love yourself." [10] Love never hurts a neighbor, so loving is obeying all the law.

Romans 13:8-10

7. How does receiving God's grace enable us to practice Christian unity and love?

_____

_____

_____

_____

_____

8. Why is it often more challenging to love the people closest to us?

_____

_____

_____

_____

_____

9. What can people outside of the church learn from the way believers get along?

_____

_____

_____

_____

_____

My Reflections

"Unity creates belief. Disunity fosters disbelief. Who wants to board a ship of bickering sailors? Life on the ocean may be rough, but at least the waves don't call us names. . . . Could it be that unity is the key to reaching the world for Christ?"—Max

Journal

In what relationship do I need to foster an attitude of love and unity? How?

_____

_____

_____

_____

_____

_____

_____

_____

_____

_____

_____

107

For Further Study

To learn more about getting along with others, read Psalm 133:1-3;
John 13:34-35; John 17:20-23; Colossians 3:12-14.

Additional Questions

10. If we are the army of Christ, what does division among the ranks
cost us?

_____

_____

_____

_____

_____

11. In your own words, what does it mean to love someone unconditionally?

_____

_____

_____

_____

_____

_____

12. If we have not truly received God's grace, what does that mean for our relationships?

_____

_____

_____

_____

_____

_____

Additional Thoughts

_____

_____

_____

_____

_____

_____

_____

_____

_____

_____

How Far Is Too Far?

"*G*od is for us.

God *is* for us.

God is *for* us.

God is for *us*."

—*Max Lucado*

1. Think of someone who stayed by you during a dark time in your life. What did that person's support mean to you?

_____

_____

_____

_____

_____

_____

_____

A Moment with Max

Max shares these insights with us in his book *In the Grip of Grace.*

There it is. This is the question. Here is what we want to know. We want to know how long God's love will endure. Paul could have begun with this one. Does God really love us forever? Not just on Easter Sunday when our shoes are shined and our hair is fixed. We want to know (deep within, don't we really want to know?), how does God feel about me when I'm a jerk? Not when I'm peppy and positive and ready to tackle world hunger. Not then. I know how he feels about me then. Even I like me then.

I want to know how he feels about me when I snap at anything that moves, when my thoughts are gutter-level, when my tongue is sharp enough to slice a rock. How does he feel about me then?

Did I drift too far? Wait too long? Slip too much?

That's what we want to know.

Can anything separate us from the love Christ has for us?

2. How does it feel to know someone will love you even on your worst day?

_____

_____

_____

_____

_____

3. What convinces you of the unconditional love Christ has for you?

_____

_____

_____

_____

_____

A Message from the Word

[31] So what should we say about this? If God is with us, no one can defeat us. [32] He did not spare his own Son but gave him for us all. So with Jesus, God will surely give us all things. [33] Who can accuse the people God has chosen? No one, because God is the One who makes them right. [34] Who can say God's people are guilty? No one, because Christ Jesus died, but he was also raised from the dead, and now he is on God's right side, begging God for us. [35] Can anything separate us from the love Christ has for us? Can troubles or problems or sufferings or hunger or nakedness or danger or violent death? [36] As it is written in the Scriptures:

"For you we are in danger of death all the time.
People think we are worth no more than sheep to be killed."

[37] But in all these things we have full victory through God who showed his love for us. [38] Yes, I am sure that neither death, nor life, nor angels, nor ruling spirits, nothing now, nothing in the future, no powers, [39] nothing above us, nothing below us, nor anything else in the whole world will ever be able to separate us from the love of God that is in Christ Jesus our Lord.

Romans 8:31-39

4. In what circumstances do we tend to doubt God's love for us? Why?

_____

_____

_____

_____

_____

_____

5. How does a deep-rooted belief in God's unconditional love for us contribute to healthy relationships with others?

_____

_____

_____

_____

_____

6. In what concrete ways can we help others understand and experience God's love?

_____

_____

_____

_____

_____

_____

More from the Word

[1] Lord, you have examined me
and know all about me.
[2] You know when I sit down and when I get up.
You know my thoughts before I think them.
[3] You know where I go and where I lie down.
You know thoroughly everything I do.

⁴ Lord, even before I say a word,
    you already know it.
⁵ You are all around me—in front and in back—
    and have put your hand on me.
⁶ Your knowledge is amazing to me;
    it is more than I can understand.
⁷ Where can I go to get away from your Spirit?
    Where can I run from you?
⁸ If I go up to the heavens, you are there.
    If I lie down in the grave, you are there.
⁹ If I rise with the sun in the east
    and settle in the west beyond the sea,
¹⁰ even there you would guide me.
    With your right hand you would hold me.

Psalm 139:1-10

7. Why do we try to hide our shortcomings from God—the only one who can help us overcome them?

_____

_____

_____

_____

_____

_____

8. How do you feel when you think of God's constant watch over you?

_____

_____

_____

9. How can you remind yourself of God's love and presence the next time you feel lonely and unlovable?

_____

_____

_____

_____

_____

My Reflections

" 'You wonder how long my love will last? Find your answer on a splintered cross, on a craggy hill. That's me you see up there, your maker, your God, nail-stabbed and bleeding. Covered in spit and sin-soaked. That's your sin I'm feeling. That's your death I'm dying. That's your resurrection I'm living. That's how much I love you.'

" 'Can anything come between you and me?' asks the firstborn Son."—Max

Journal

What have I allowed to come between my Savior and me? How can I eliminate the things that interfere with our relationship?

For Further Study

To learn more about God's unfailing love, read Isaiah 54:10; Jeremiah 31:3; John 3:16–17; Ephesians 3:17–19; 1 John 3:1.

Additional Questions

10. Why do we sometimes find it difficult to love ourselves even though a perfect and holy God loves us?

_____

_____

_____

_____

_____

11. Describe a person who has shown you unconditional love. How can you imitate that person?

_____

_____

_____

_____

_____

_____

12. How can God's love give you courage to face the obstacles and trials in your life?

_____

_____

_____

_____

Additional Thoughts

_____

_____

_____

_____

_____

_____

_____

_____

_____

_____